God Loves Me!

Written by Karen Rhodes
Illustrated by Jane Dippold

Warner
Press Kids
educate • nurture • inspire
www.warnerpress.org

30580028959

God loves ME! WOW!
My eyes may be brown,
blue or green.
My hair may be red,
black, blonde or brown.
My skin may be brown,
black or white.
It doesn't matter
because God loves me
just the way I am!

How do I know God loves me?

His Word, the Bible, tells me:

I have loved thee [you] with an everlasting love.

(Jeremiah 31:3)

Everlasting means always, forever.

God loved me when I was just a baby.

He loves me now, and He will love me when I'm older.

How does God
show me His love?
He gives me
a beautiful world to live in.
I have trees to climb
or to sit under.

Pretty flowers of red, yellow, blue, orange, purple—
all kinds of colors are made by God.
He made them smell good too.
Hmmmm!

God gives us animals to love and they love us back.
I have a puppy that likes to play ball,
and a kitten that likes to sit on my lap.

Mommy and Daddy love me,
and so do my sister and brother.
I love them too!
God's love is shared in families.

I have a nice house,
a swing set and friends
who come over to play
and have a good time.

My family enjoys eating together.
We thank God for the food He gives us.
We talk about all the things we've done that day.

I feel God's love the most
when I go to church.
Our pastor is so kind.
He shakes my hand,
looks me in the eye,
and tells me he's glad to see me.

I love to go to Sunday school!
We listen to stories about Jesus,
color pictures and sing.
My teacher is so nice!
I know she loves me too.

I feel God's love
in the heat of the sun.
I love hot days when our family goes
to the beach to play in the water
and to build sandcastles.

God is so neat!
He also gives us cold days to play in the snow.
I love the snow!
It's so white and clean.

In Sunday school we hear,

*For God so loved the world,
that he gave his only begotten Son...*

WOW! God loves us so much He
sent Jesus to die on the cross—
for ME and for YOU!

that whosoever believeth in him should not perish, but have everlasting life.
(John 3:16)

God wants me (and you)
to love Him back.
If I love Him,
I'll go to heaven when I die.

God's love is everywhere.
He loves everybody—all over the world.
That's a lot of people. And He loves ME!